MIGRANTS

Eduard Altarriba

BUTTON BOOKS

**Give me your tired, your poor,
Your huddled masses yearning to breathe free**

Emma Lazarus
"The New Colossus"
Quoted on the plaque in the base Statue of Liberty

Contents

HUMANITY HAS ALWAYS MOVED

The first humans were hunter-gatherers who lived in small nomadic groups which followed the migration paths of the animals they hunted. The development of agriculture meant that most societies became settled in one place. Yet humans continued to move around the planet, sometimes in search of a better life, and sometimes fleeing war or natural disasters.

MORE THAN A MILLION YEARS AGO

During the Paleolithic period, the first early humans came out of Africa and settled in Europe and Asia.

MORE THAN 50,000 YEARS AGO

Various groups of *Homo sapiens* (our own species) migrated from Africa and spread out across the whole world: Europe, Asia, Australia, Oceania, and even across the Bering Strait to the Americas.

ABOUT 12,000 YEARS AGO

During the "Neolithic Revolution," people learned how to grow crops and agriculture developed. This meant that millions of people stopped being nomadic and stayed in one place instead.

ABOUT 6,000 YEARS AGO

People living in the Americas had no contact with other continents. The growth of great empires, such as the Incas, the Mayans, and the Aztecs, led to big migrations of people.

BETWEEN THE 3RD AND 7TH CENTURIES

People in the colder regions of Europe and Asia moved south to the territories of the Roman, Persian, and Gupta (in India) empires. The Romans called these migratory movements "barbarian invasions."

BETWEEN THE 9TH AND 20TH CENTURIES

In Europe during this time, there were many wars, invasions, plagues, and famines that caused massive displacements of people.

WHAT ARE
BORDERS?

They are imaginary lines that separate countries. Each country has its own type of government, laws, and taxes, and sets itself apart from other countries through symbols such as flags or national anthems.

People and **goods** have to cross borders to get from one country to another. Each country has **laws** that say who and what can enter its territory. The **police**, the **military**, and **customs officials** make sure these laws are followed by keeping watch over their country's borders.

WHY ARE BORDERS WHERE THEY ARE?

Borders have changed many, many times over the course of history.

Some societies have lived separated by natural borders: deserts, mountains, rivers, or seas.

Inheritances and royal marriages have united and separated nations.

Invasions and wars have often led to borders changing.

In the 19th and 20th centuries, European countries invaded and shared out much of Asia and Africa, inventing countries that did not exist before.

PASSPORTS AND VISAS

In order to cross a border legally and enter a country, people need a number of documents. The most important one is a PASSPORT, but sometimes people also need a VISA.

When you enter a country (at a border crossing, port, or airport), the police in that country ask you to show your passport and, if necessary, your visa. If you do not have these documents, you will not be allowed to enter the country.

THERE ARE PEOPLE WHO HAVE MORE THAN ONE NATIONALITY, SO THEY CAN HAVE MORE THAN ONE PASSPORT.

A passport is a document that can only be used by the person who holds it. It is very difficult to forge.

A VISA is a permit given by the country you want to enter. The visa states how, when, and why a person can enter a country. There are visas that allow you to enter as a tourist for a few weeks, and visas that allow you to stay in the country to live and work.

HOW DO YOU GET THE DOCUMENTS YOU NEED TO ENTER A COUNTRY?

Who DOES NOT have problems crossing borders?

Generally speaking, rich people, highly educated people, and those who live in rich countries have few problems going from one country to another.

UK and US citizens can visit the following countries without a visa: Albania, Antigua and Barbuda, Argentina, Armenia, Austria, Bahamas, Barbados, Belgium, Belize, Bosnia and Herzegovina, Botswana, Brazil, Brunei, Bulgaria, Cape Verde, Chile, Colombia, Costa Rica, Croatia, Cyprus, Czechia, Denmark, Dominica, Dominican Republic, Ecuador, El Salvador, Estonia, Eswatini, Fiji, Finland, France, Georgia, Germany, Greece, Grenada, Guatemala, Guyana, Haiti, Honduras, Hong Kong, Hungary, Iceland, Ireland, Israel, Italy, Jamaica, Kazakhstan, Kiribati, Kosovo, Kyrgyzstan, Latvia, Lesotho, Liechtenstein, Lithuania, Luxembourg, Malaysia, Malta, Marshall Islands, Mauritius, Mexico, Micronesia, Moldova, Monaco, Montenegro, Morocco, Namibia, Netherlands, Nicaragua, North Macedonia, Norway, Palestinian Territories, Panama, Paraguay, Peru, Philippines, Poland, Portugal, Qatar, Romania, Saint Kitts and Nevis, Saint Lucia, San Marino, St. Vincent and the Grenadines, Sao Tome and Principe, Senegal, Serbia, Singapore, Slovakia, Slovenia, South Africa, Spain, Sweden, Switzerland, Taiwan, Thailand, Trinidad and Tobago, Tunisia, Ukraine, Uruguay, Vanuatu, and the Vatican City. UK citizens can also visit Belarus, Bolivia, Gambia, Turkey, Uzbekistan, Venezuela, and Vietnam without a visa (but not the US), and US citizens can visit Canada, Central African Republic, Equatorial Guinea, Mongolia, Palau, Tajikistan, and the UK without a visa.

Who DOES have problems crossing borders?

People who live in poor countries have the most problems getting documents and visas to cross borders.

If you have a passport from Afghanistan you can visit Dominica, Haiti, and Micronesia without a visa.

You can compare passports and entitlements by country on https://www.passportindex.org

European colonization

From the 15th century onward, European explorers opened up new sea routes around the globe, claiming any lands they found for their own country—even if other people already lived there. In time, new technologies such as steamships helped to create transport networks that connected the world's oceans. This allowed massive migrations of people across the seas.

European countries such as Spain, France, Great Britain, Portugal, and the Netherlands conquered half the world, setting up colonies in the Americas, Africa, India, Southeast Asia, Australia, the Pacific, and elsewhere.

From the 16th to the 19th centuries, European colonial countries enslaved more than 10 million African people. These people were put on boats and forced to leave their lives behind and work as slaves on plantations in the Americas, on the other side of the Atlantic Ocean. The work done by enslaved people helped to make the USA and the colonial countries very rich.

The African slave trade to the Americas was the biggest forced migration in history.

Colonization also led to the movement of many European people. Many European settlers started living in the conquered territories, even though they were already inhabited by other people. In the 19th century, around 38 million Europeans settled in the new colonies.

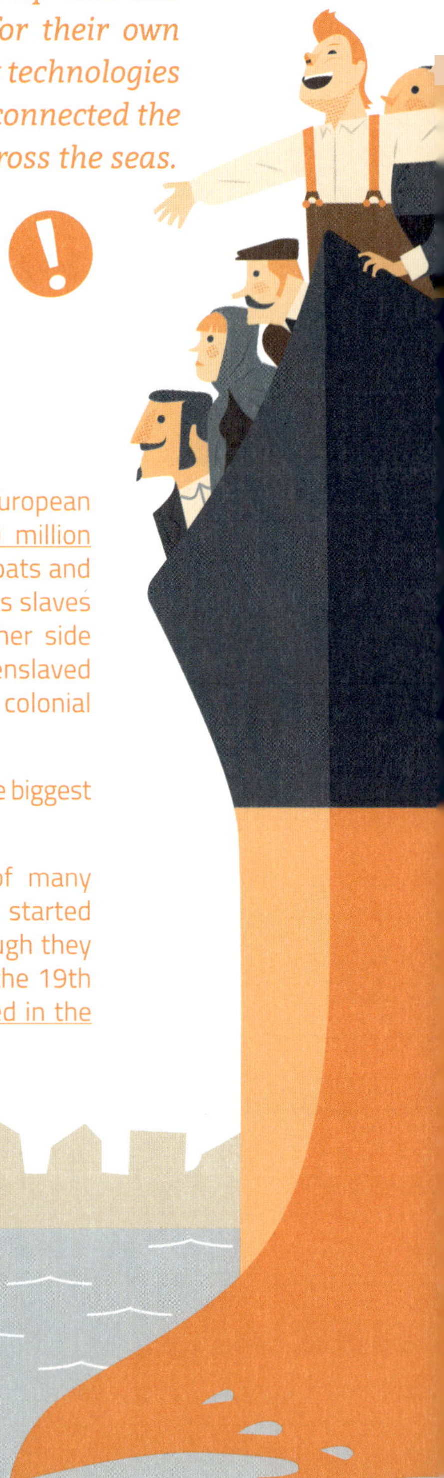

By the mid-19th century, most of the Americas had gained independence from the colonial countries.

The USA, which declared its independence in 1776, based its new identity on immigrants. Millions upon millions of Europeans arrived in the USA, fleeing hunger and poverty. They imagined America to be the "land of opportunity," a place where they could start new lives.

The indigenous Native American people who had lived in America for thousands of years were almost exterminated, and their land was filled with white Europeans.

See "Land of Immigrants," page 38

Who can migrate?

Not everyone is able to migrate. As we have seen, people need the right documents (such as a visa and passport) to cross a border legally.

When this is not possible, people who want to go to another country have to pay a lot of money to criminals called traffickers, who smuggle them across the border illegally.

Often families borrow money so they can pay for one of their family members to travel to another country. They hope that when this person arrives at their destination, they will find work and be able to repay the debt.

But the very poorest people (a large part of humanity) have no way of either getting the documents they need or raising the money to pay for the journey. Their only option is to migrate to cities in their own country to seek new opportunities.

Where to go?

The vast majority of people want to go to rich countries, where they believe they will have more opportunities to find a good job and succeed economically and socially.

That is why richer countries, such as the USA, the countries in the European Union, or the Arab states of the Persian Gulf tend to be the preferred destination for thousands of people across the planet.

MAIN MIGRANT

DESPITE THE OBSTACLES TO MIGRATION THAT SOME COUNTRIES PUT IN PLACE, MILLIONS OF PEOPLE HAVE MIGRATED LEGALLY SINCE THE MID-20TH CENTURY. THESE ARE SOME OF THE MAIN MIGRANT ROUTES SINCE 1990.

The population of the European Union is around 450 million people.

In Europe, citizens of countries that have signed the Schengen agreement can move freely from one country to another within the Schengen area.

See page 34

The Nicaraguan government spends $59 per person per year on education.

The population of Nigeria is 217 million people, slightly more than the total number of people living in France, Spain, and Germany. Every year, Nigeria's population increases by 5.5 million.

Sources: unfpa.org // worldbank.org

Not all migrant routes cross borders between countries. Millions of people move from the countryside to cities in Africa, Asia, South America, and Central America. It is estimated that by 2050, two out of every three people will be living in a city.

Source: population.un.org/wup/

ROUTES (Since 1990)

Source: iom.int

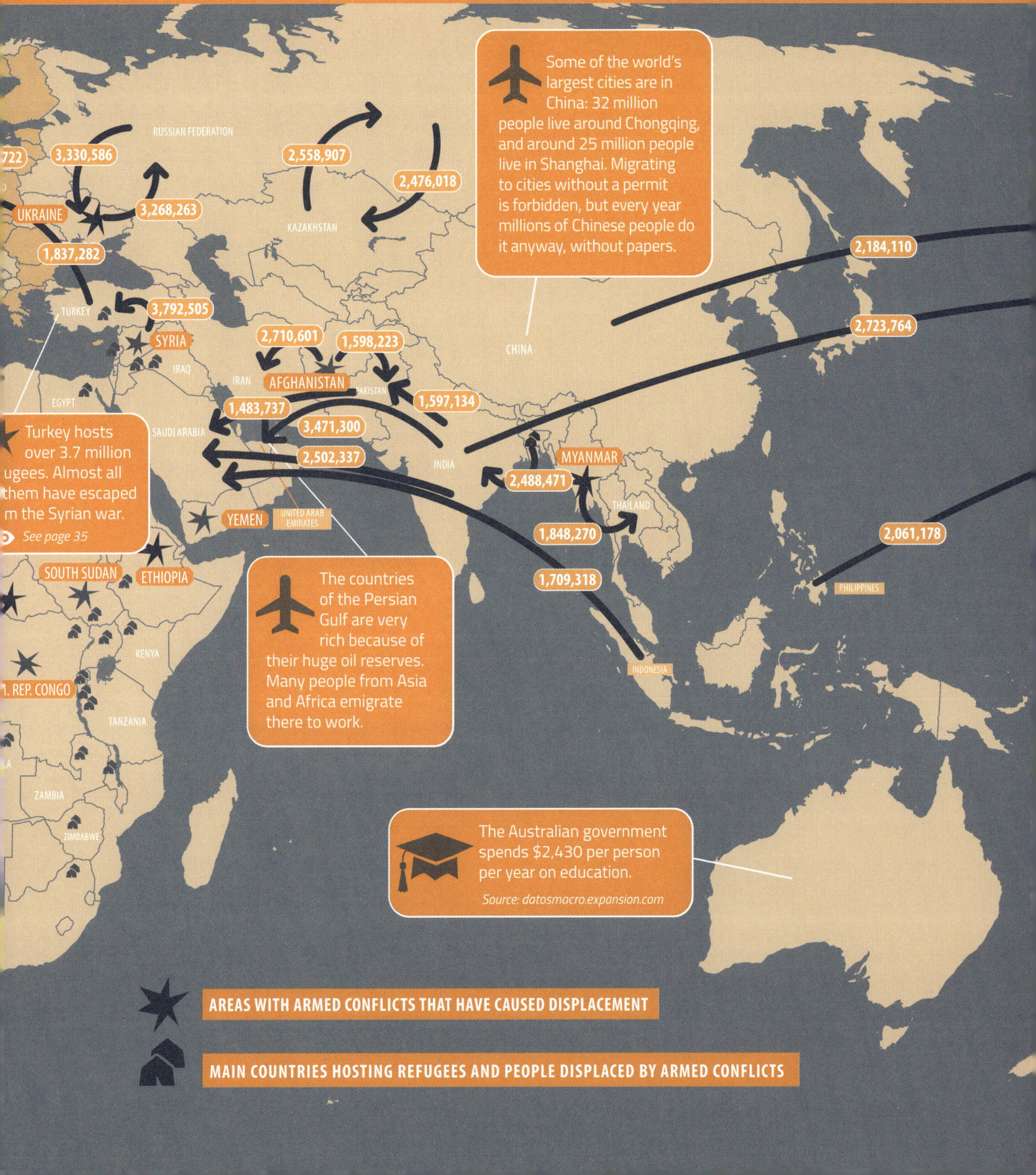

Some of the world's largest cities are in China: 32 million people live around Chongqing, and around 25 million people live in Shanghai. Migrating to cities without a permit is forbidden, but every year millions of Chinese people do it anyway, without papers.

Turkey hosts over 3.7 million ugees. Almost all them have escaped m the Syrian war.

See page 35

The countries of the Persian Gulf are very rich because of their huge oil reserves. Many people from Asia and Africa emigrate there to work.

The Australian government spends $2,430 per person per year on education.

Source: datosmacro.expansion.com

AREAS WITH ARMED CONFLICTS THAT HAVE CAUSED DISPLACEMENT

MAIN COUNTRIES HOSTING REFUGEES AND PEOPLE DISPLACED BY ARMED CONFLICTS

WHY DO PEOPLE MIGRATE?

It is not easy leaving your home, your family, and your friends. There are many things that drive people to emigrate: war, insecurity, work. But most people leave their homes for economic reasons.

Poverty

Many people live in places where there is very little work and few opportunities to study. Sometimes they do not have basic services like electricity, drinking water, medicines, and healthcare. So some people leave, often for big cities or other countries, looking for a place where they can find work and make money, so they can help their families.

➡ In the Philippines, for example, emigrants are called *bagong bayani* ("the new heroes"), because the money they send home not only helps their family, but also the whole country's economy.

Natural disasters

Climate change and pollution are bringing about big changes in many areas of the planet, from rising sea levels to desertification (the turning of fertile land into desert).

Natural disasters such as earthquakes, tsunamis, and wildfires also cause many people to flee their homes.

In some countries, such as the Bahamas, Maldives, Vanuatu, Fiji, and Jamaica, the sea level is rising rapidly and entire populations are having to abandon their coastal towns.

What happens if these countries disappear?

Even today the law does not recognize climate or environmental refugees. There is no protection for anyone forcibly displaced due to climate-related causes.

Persecution

Many people have to flee their countries because of their political opinions, ideas, religion, or sexuality, or because they belong to a particular ethnic group.

Fleeing war

If you live in a place where there is an armed conflict, you might be shot, your neighborhood might be bombed or your house destroyed. Food and medicine are in short supply, hospitals are overcrowded, and stores are closed. Your life, your family's lives, and your friends' lives are in great danger. That is why people flee war.

WHERE DO REFUGEES FLEEING WAR COME FROM?

Syria, Ukraine, Afghanistan, South Sudan, Sahel, Yemen, Central African Republic, Nigeria, Burundi, Somalia, Ethiopia, and Democratic Republic of the Congo.

2022 data

AR 345

REFUGEES

UNIVERSAL DECLARATION OF HUMAN RIGHTS

Since the Second World War, most of the world's countries have agreed to a set of international rules to prevent humanitarian disasters like those seen during that terrible war.

All these countries signed the **Universal Declaration of Human Rights** (UDHR), which sets out fundamental human rights that must always be respected under all circumstances.

RIGHT TO ASYLUM

One of the fundamental rights in the UDHR is **the right to asylum or international protection**: if a person is persecuted in their own country, they can request protection from any other country in the world.

When a country agrees to protect a person, it gives them **refugee status**. This lasts for the person's entire life: no one can ever take it away.

But, what does being persecuted mean? A person can request asylum when they can prove they are being treated badly because of their ethnicity, religion, gender, sexuality, or nationality, or for their political opinions or for belonging to a particular social group*.

* The Convention Relating to the Status of Refugees is the document that explains who has the right to request asylum.

International laws are supposed to protect every person on the planet equally. But each country applies the laws in different ways and sometimes simply ignores them.

When a person requests asylum FROM A FOREIGN GOVERNMENT, it is the start of a long process that varies according to each country's laws. Obtaining ASYLUM is very complicated because there are very strict conditions that need to be met, and many asylum seekers are unable to gather the evidence needed to prove they are being persecuted in their own country.

DISPLACED AND INTERNALLY DISPLACED PERSONS

DISPLACED PERSONS *are people who have had to flee their homes, mainly because of armed conflict or natural disasters.*

Most end up in camps in countries bordering the conflict zone, such as Iran, Lebanon, Pakistan, or Turkey. Life is hard in these camps.

INTERNALLY DISPLACED PERSONS *are people who have had to flee their homes, but have not crossed their country's borders.*

By the end of 2021 there were around 55 million internally displaced people in the world, many in countries with armed conflicts, such as Afghanistan, Colombia, the Democratic Republic of Congo, and Iraq.

DISPLACED PERSONS AND REFUGEES, 2021

89.3 million DISPLACED PERSONS

27.1 million REFUGEES

4.6 million ASYLUM SEEKERS

TRAFFICKERS

When people who want to migrate to another country cannot get the necessary visas and permits to cross the border, they look for other ways to enter. Their only option is to use unofficial routes, but these are difficult and dangerous. Gangs of organized criminals called traffickers control the illegal entry routes into countries. Migrants have to pay these traffickers a lot of money to cross the borders unofficially.

Traffickers use many methods to cross borders: they use land and sea routes, forge documents, bribe government officials, and hide people in cargo containers.

The traffickers often rob, cheat, and exploit migrants. Sometimes they use threats and violence to force the migrants to work for them, even after they have settled in the new country.

In summary . . .

Never in the history of humanity has it been so easy, quick, and cheap to travel.

Never before have so many people been able to move from one place to another on our planet.

PEOPLE ON THE MOVE

But visiting somewhere as a tourist for a few days or going to work for a few years in a place where you have a guaranteed job is not the same as having to flee your home because your life is in danger.

TOURISTS

People who make the most of their vacation to discover places and cultures different from their own.

EXPATRIATES

People who choose to work in another country for a few years, legally and usually with a guaranteed job. For example, managers of multinational companies, international government officials, or employees of non-governmental organizations (NGOs).

MIGRANTS

People who leave their homes to seek a better future or to flee danger.

PEOPLE MOVING TO FLEE DANGER

People who have to flee their homes due to danger, such as war, a natural disaster, or persecution.

REFUGEES

People who have requested, and been given, asylum in another country and so have refugee status.

INTERNALLY DISPLACED PERSONS

People who have had to flee their homes, mainly because of armed conflict, violence, or natural disaster, but who have not left their country.

DISPLACED PERSONS

People who have had to flee their countries, mainly because of armed conflict, violence, or natural disaster, but who have not requested or been given refugee status.

It is very difficult for all those who do not have recognized refugee status (whether they cross an international border or not) to access basic rights like education, healthcare, work, and freedom to move around.

PEOPLE MOVING FOR ECONOMIC REASONS

People who leave their homes in search of a better future, either in their own country or abroad.

ILLEGAL MIGRANTS

People who have migrated to a country and settled there without the necessary permits.

LEGAL MIGRANTS

People who have the necessary documents and permits to leave their countries and live in a different one, either permanently or for a long time.

There are people who don't like immigrants* coming to their country.

There are people who love their country very much and who don't like things to change.

People who are afraid their country will fill up with poor people from other cultures and religions.

People who are afraid that all these people coming from far away are a threat to their customs and traditions.

People who are afraid they will become the minority in their own country.

People who are afraid that immigrants will bring crime and problems.

---

*The word migrant means anyone who migrates. We use the word immigrant to refer to those arriving in a new country. Emigrants refers to those leaving a country to settle elsewhere.

Xenophobic parties

Xenophobia is a dislike or fear of anything that is foreign, especially people. In rich countries that welcome immigration, there are xenophobic political parties that exploit people's fears to win votes. These nationalist parties want to expel immigrants and refugees, and close the border so they are not able to enter.

However, there are also many people who believe that diversity, different customs, and different religions bring cultural richness and positive values.

People who believe that all people should have the same rights, wherever they come from and wherever they end up.

People who are more concerned about why some people are forced to leave their homes to seek a better future in another country.

It's not easy for immigrants to go and live in a new place with a different culture and language, especially when they are poorer than most people. It's also not easy for the people in the host society, who might not like lots of people arriving who have different customs and religions to them.

Because immigrants can find it difficult to relate to the host society, they sometimes group together in neighborhoods where they feel more comfortable. But this isolates them from the rest of society.

To break down these barriers between communities, everyone needs to make an effort. People in the host society need to accept that people live differently, and immigrants who have just arrived need to make an effort to integrate into the host country and respect its customs.

"First-generation immigrants" are people who emigrate to settle in a new host country. Their children and grandchildren (the second and third generations) are born and raised in the new country, and so gradually take on more of the culture of the host country and become separated from their grandparents' original culture.

FILE

THE MIGRANT CRISIS IN THE MEDITERRANEAN

Since 2014, European Union (EU) border officials have detected around 4 million people attempting to enter Europe illegally with the aim of requesting asylum. The European Union has responded to this migration by reinforcing its borders.

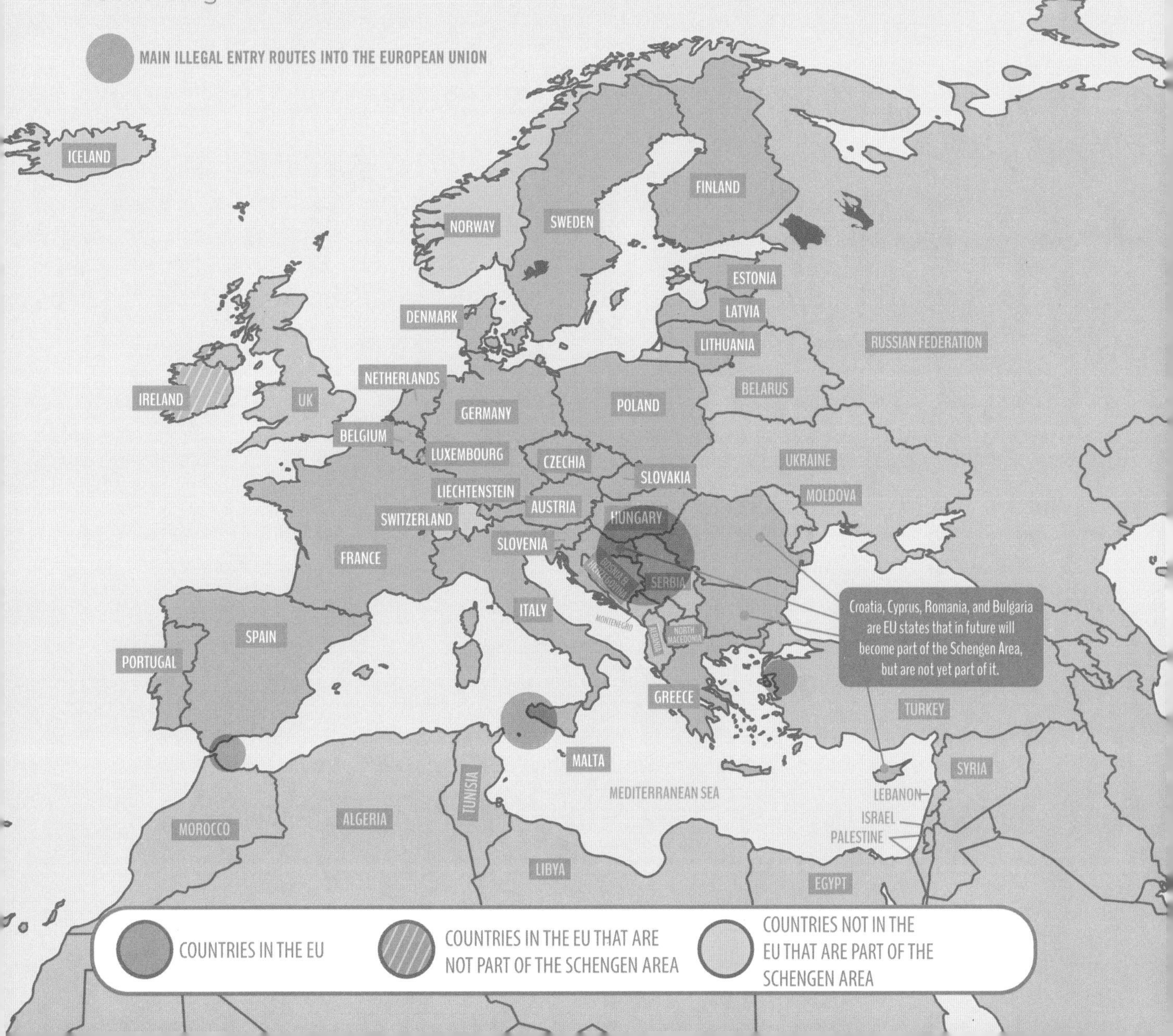

WHY EUROPE?

Thousands and thousands of people try to reach the European Union to escape poverty and wars. But why Europe? European countries are some of the richest in the world and have healthcare, education, legal protection, and other systems that other countries lack. They are also very safe. That is why migrants want to live in these countries.

But many of these migrants do not have a visa to enter the European Union. They hope to reach Europe so they can apply for asylum or, at least, remain there illegally until they can find a way of making their situation legal. As they cannot legally enter the European Union, they look for other routes controlled by traffickers, some of which are very dangerous.

WHAT IS THE SCHENGEN AREA?

The EUROPEAN UNION is the political and economic alliance of nearly all the countries in mainland Europe. Most of these countries have the same currency, the euro, and nearly all of them have signed up to the Schengen agreement, which abolishes border controls and allows people and goods to move around freely from one country to another within the European Union.*

Migrants know that if they reach one country in the European Union they can request refugee status, and while the process is going on, they will not be expelled from the EU. Meanwhile, they will look for a way to stay in Europe, even if it is illegal. Because they are free to move around within the Schengen area, they will try to reach the country where they want to settle.

*There are European countries, such as the United Kingdom and Ireland, that are not in the Schengen area. Other countries, like Iceland and Norway, are not in the European Union but have signed the Schengen agreement.

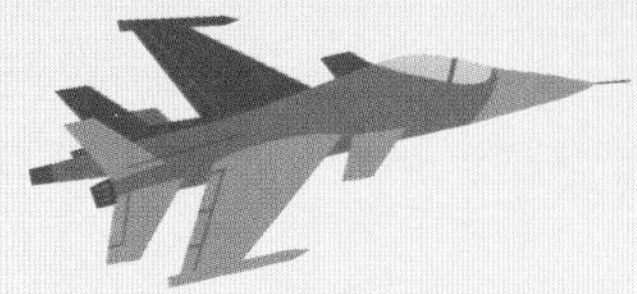

The refugee problem

The richest countries in Europe, such as France, the United Kingdom, and Germany, are the preferred destinations for migrants. These countries, especially those which once had colonies in Africa and Asia, have historically accepted immigrants.

But the sudden arrival of a large number of people poses a problem for governments, as they have to deal with asylum applications and make sure basic services are in place for all the new arrivals. This is why European countries would prefer an orderly entry of immigrants rather than a massive influx.

Also, the arrival of lots of immigrants is unpopular with much of the population. This leads to the rise of extreme political parties, who call for the closing of borders and even expelling foreigners.

THE WAR IN SYRIA

Since 2011, there has been a civil war in Syria, which has led to thousands of casualties and millions of displaced persons. Many of those who fled the Syrian civil war now live in refugee camps in Lebanon and Turkey, but many others have tried to reach Europe.

The Balkans is a mountain range stretching from Greece to Austria. Many of the refugees fleeing Syria arrived in the European Union on foot, first crossing Turkey and then moving up toward central Europe through the countries around the Balkans.

See the book *What is War?* in the same series

EUROPE CLOSES ITS BORDERS

In 2016, European Union governments decided they would no longer allow the large numbers of refugees entering Europe illegally.

Countries such as Hungary and Bulgaria reinforced their borders with fences and police. The European Union also came to an agreement with Turkey: in exchange for significant economic benefits, the Turkish government would stop the movement of migrants through Turkey. Migrants who arrive illegally in Greece are sent back to Turkey, where they are housed in refugee camps.

As a result of this, fewer migrants traveled via the Balkans route and the Eastern Mediterranean route (see below). However, new routes to Europe were created.

CEUTA AND MELILLA

These two cities are on the coast of Morocco in North Africa, but belong to Spain (and are therefore European Union territory). This makes them a goal for many emigrants from Africa. But the Spanish authorities have erected some huge, patrolled fences around the two cities, which are very difficult and dangerous to cross.

Migrants using the Eastern Mediterranean route travel by sea from Turkey to Greece (the mainland and islands), Bulgaria, and Cyprus.

Many people can't swim and they usually wear life jackets.

It is very cold, especially in winter.

Before they reach the boat, migrants have to travel thousands of miles overland.

The only baggage allowed is a small backpack.

To make more money on each trip, traffickers squeeze as many people as they can on each boat.

But this is not the only sea route in the Mediterranean. Migrants from Africa and Asia have been crossing the Mediterranean Sea to try and reach Europe for many years.

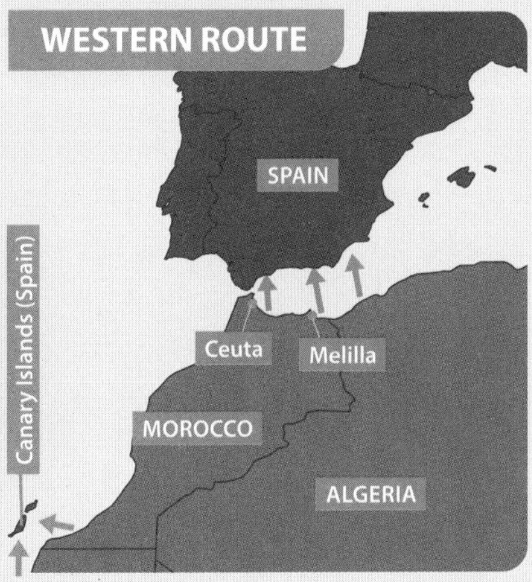

LIBYA

Years ago there was a civil war in Libya in North Africa, and today the country is still divided into territories controlled by different armed groups. The absence of laws and police make it a perfect place to try to cross the Mediterranean Sea. But it is also a very dangerous place where traffickers can abuse migrants without fear of being punished.

Traffickers control the illegal sea routes across the Mediterranean Sea. Migrants have to pay a lot of money for a place on a flimsy boat and take a very, very dangerous journey. Many never make it to Europe.

Maritime laws say that if a ship spots a boat sinking, it has to rescue the victims and take them to a safe port. Many migrants hope to be rescued and taken to Europe, but they are often sent back to Turkey or Lebanon.

Boat journeys are done at night to avoid being spotted by coastguards. If migrants are seen before reaching European waters, they can be forced to turn back.

Sometimes, it is the migrants themselves who have to steer the boat. It is easy to get lost at sea and suffer thirst and hunger.

Some non-governmental organizations, such as Open Arms, rescue migrant boats drifting in the Mediterranean Sea, although governments are making it more and more difficult for them to do this.

REFUGEE CAMPS

The European Union does not want immigrants who arrive on European shores to be able to move around freely within the Schengen area. So migrant camps have been set up in places like the Greek island of Lesbos, where immigrants have to stay until a decision is made about whether or not they will be given refugee status. Those who are not given refugee status are deported to Turkey.

FILE

Migrant caravans to the UNITED STATES

For many years, migrants have traveled up from Central America through Mexico to try to reach the USA. Many chose to travel in groups called caravans to make the journey safer.

STATIONS OF THE CROSS CARAVAN

In March 2018, more than 700 migrants from Central America decided to leave together from Tapachula, Mexico, in an attempt to reach the USA and claim asylum from the violence in their countries of origin. As the caravan grew in size to over 1,200 people, the US president, Donald Trump, threatened to send the army to the southern border and rip up the special trade agreement between Mexico, the USA, and Canada. This caravan, called the "Stations of the Cross," attracted attention from around the world, mainly because of Trump's declarations. Other caravans followed later that year.

LAND OF IMMIGRANTS

The growth of the USA has been due to its millions of immigrants.

In the USA, as in many places that have welcomed immigration, the immigrants who arrived first and have lived there for generations believe they have more rights than those who have arrived more recently.

18th century The USA declared independence from Great Britain in 1776.

At the time of independence, the USA was home to English, French, and Spanish settlers living on the East Coast on land that belonged to the indigenous Native American people. This was also the era of slavery, which brought millions of African people to work in plantations in the southern colonies (see page 12).

19th century

From the 19th century, migrants to the USA came mainly from Germany, Ireland, and other northern European countries. Within the USA, millions of people moved steadily westward, colonizing new indigenous land. In the south, part of Mexico was annexed, bringing a large Hispanic community within the USA's borders.

"Melting pot" is an expression used to explain that the USA is a country made up of people from all over the world.

20th century | SECOND WORLD WAR | 1965* | 21st century

Around the turn of the 20th century, most migrants to the USA were people from countries in southern and eastern Europe, who were often fleeing wars and revolutions.

After the Second World War, the USA welcomed many people from Asia (especially India, the Philippines, and China) and South America, who wanted to escape the poverty and violence of their own countries. In the 21st century, people continue to arrive from all over the world.

*The 1965 Immigration Act made it very difficult to become an American citizen if you had no family in the country or if you weren't a highly qualified professional or if you didn't have refugee status.

A DANGEROUS JOURNEY

For many years, thousands and thousands of Central Americans have believed that life in the USA is much better than in their own countries, and they are willing to do anything to get there.

WHAT ARE THEY RUNNING AWAY FROM?

Countries in Central America have many problems related to insecurity, poverty, corruption, and environmental disasters.

Since the civil wars and dictatorships of the 20th century, the region has had a terrible history of domestic, social, and political violence. Governments and the police have frequently been linked with crime and corruption, which has left the population feeling unprotected.

The "maras" are gangs of extremely violent criminals involved in extortion, theft, and murder. Entire neighborhoods live in fear, without the police doing much to deal with it.

CROSSING MEXICO

The journey to the USA crosses Mexico, where migrants run the risk of being robbed, kidnapped, assaulted, or even killed if they attempt to travel without the help of a smuggler. Hiring a smuggler can cost between 2,000 and 10,000 US dollars.

As a result, many migrants get together and travel in groups called caravans, as this is much safer than traveling alone. In late 2018, a number of caravans set out from Central America, and at least 6,000 migrants, including over 1,000 children, crossed Mexico to reach the US border.

Donald Trump won the USA presidential election in 2016 mainly on the issue of immigration. Trump did not want more immigrants to enter the USA and pushed policies to limit or block legal entry routes into the country, including applying for asylum.

One of Trump's election promises was to build a wall along the 2,000-mile-long (3,150 km) border between Mexico and the USA to keep out illegal immigrants. Although many of the people in the caravans wanted to live elsewhere in Mexico and did not try to enter the USA, Trump continued to use immigrants to justify the need to build his wall.

Some migrants choose to pay for the services of traffickers called "coyotes," who know illegal entry routes across the desert. People who use these routes face the danger of getting lost in the desert and dying of thirst. They also have to avoid getting caught by the US border guard patrols (sometimes assisted by soldiers and the National Guard) and the armed American civilians who want to stop migrants entering the country.

LIFE AS AN ILLEGAL

People who manage to enter the USA illegally are forced to live in hiding.

They survive by taking insecure jobs with very low wages, and they always run the risk of being discovered by "la migra" (the US immigration enforcement officials) and expelled from the country.

GLOSSARY

annex
To take over an area of land or country, usually without permission and using force.

asylum
Protection offered by a country to someone being persecuted by their own country. The person who is applying for asylum is called an **asylum seeker**.

bribe
To try and persuade somebody to do something, by offering money or other favors.

caravan
A group of people traveling together. The term is used to describe the groups of migrants who travel by foot from Central and South America to the Mexico-US border in order to gain entry to the US.

citizen
A person who legally belongs to a country and has the rights and protection of that country.

civil war
A war fought within a country between different groups of citizens.

coastguard
Part of a country's military forces that is responsible for looking after the coast and carrying out rescues.

colonize
To send people to settle in another land and take control of it. The land taken is called a **colony**.

colonies
See *fiffiffiffiffiffigfi*

corruption
Dishonest or illegal behavior, where someone uses their position of power (for example, in government or the police) to benefit themselves.

customs official
A person whose job it is to collect taxes on goods coming into a country and to stop illegal goods from entering.

dictatorship
A form of government in which one person rules over a country and has absolute power. Very often these leaders aren't chosen by their people and rule very harshly, using strict laws.

displacement
The situation in which a person or people are forced to leave the place or country where they live, because of war, natural disasters, or other reasons. The people affected are called **displaced persons**.

emigrate
To leave one country and move to another. A person who emigrates is called an **emigrant**.

ethnic group
A group of people who share the same background, such as language and history.

European Union (EU)
The political and economic union of 27 countries within Europe.

extortion
A crime where a person uses force or threats to get something (such as money) from another person.

famine
A widespread shortage of food affecting a large number of people. In extreme cases, it causes starvation and death.

forge
To create an illegal or fake copy of a document.

Hispanic
A term used to describe a person who comes from Spain or a Spanish-speaking country in South or Central America.

Homo sapiens
Modern human beings, who appeared around 300,000 to 200,000 years ago.

host
A country or society that receives people from other countries.

humanitarian disaster
An emergency that takes place when a war, natural disaster, or other event overwhelms a population and they are unable to cope.

hunter-gatherers
People who live by hunting and foraging food, instead of farming.

ID card
A card that gives a person's name, photograph, and other information. In some countries, people have to carry their ID cards to prove who they are.

immigrant
A person who moves to another country to live there permanently.

indigenous
The first people to live in a place, such as Native American people in the United States.

inheritance
Objects, property, and money that a person receives after someone dies.

insecurity
The term used to describe when a person does not feel safe from threats such as hunger, disease, crime, or poverty.

integrate
To bring together and combine thoroughly.

internally displaced person
A person who has been forced to leave their home but hasn't left their home country.

maritime law
The laws that relate to ships and the transport of goods across the seas.

migrate
To move from one country or place to another. A person who migrates is called a **migrant**.

nationalist
Someone who strongly supports their own country, often also believing their country is better than others.

nomads
People who choose to live by moving from place to place, rather than staying in one place. This way of living is called **nomadic**.

non-governmental organizations (NGOs)
Organizations that work independently of government to support lots of different causes, from education and healthcare to women's rights and the environment.

Paleolithic period
The period of time lasting from around 2.5 million years ago to around 12,000 years ago, also known as the early Stone Age. During this time, early humans started to make and use stone tools.

persecution
Harassment or mistreatment of someone, for example because of their race, appearance, religion, or political beliefs.

plague
A infectious disease that quickly spreads to many people and often causes death.

plantations
Large pieces of land, especially in tropical countries, that grow crops such as rubber, sugar, tea, or coffee.

professionals
A person whose job requires a high level of skill, training, or education, for example, a doctor or an engineer.

refugee
A person who has been forced to leave their country to escape persecution, war, or violence.

refugee camp
Temporary camps built to provide protection and help to refugees.

refugee status
When a government officially recognizes a person is a refugee in law.

traffickers
Organized criminals who use illegal entry routes into countries to smuggle in people and illegal goods, such as drugs.

First published 2023 in English by Button Books, an imprint of Guild of Master Craftsman Publications Ltd, Castle Place, 166 High Street, Lewes, East Sussex, BN7 1XU, UK. © Eduard Altarriba, 2019. English text © GMC Publications Ltd, 2023. ISBN: 978-1-78708-129-1. Distributed by Publishers Group West in the United States. All rights reserved. This translation of *Migrants* is published by arrangement with Asterisc Agents. The right of Eduard Altarriba to be identified as the author of this work has been asserted in accordance with the Copyright, Designs and Patents Act 1988, sections 77 and 78. No part of this publication may be reproduced, stored in a retrieval system, or transmitted in any form or by any means without the prior permission of the publisher and copyright owner. While every effort has been made to obtain permission from the copyright holders for all material used in this book, the publishers will be pleased to hear from anyone who has not been appropriately acknowledged and to make the correction in future reprints. The publishers and authors can accept no legal responsibility for any consequences arising from the application of information, advice, or instructions given in this publication. A catalog record for this book is available from the British Library. For Alababalà, Editors: María Rodríguez and Amelia Fernández. For GMC Publications, Publisher: Jonathan Bailey; Production Director: Jim Bulley; Senior Project Editor: Tom Kitch; Design Manager: Robin Shields; English Translation: Andrea Reece; Editor: Claire Saunders; Publishing Assistant: Charlotte Mockridge. Color origination by GMC Reprographics. Printed and bound in Malaysia.